YA
745.5
ENZ

EDGE BOOKS™

RECYCLED science

AWESOME
CRAFT STICK
SCIENCE

BY TAMMY ENZ

Consultant:
Marcelle A. Siegel
Associate Professor of Science Education
University of Missouri

CAPSTONE PRESS
a capstone imprint

Edge Books are published by Capstone Press,
1710 Roe Crest Drive, North Mankato, Minnesota 56003
www.mycapstone.com

Library of Congress Cataloging-in-Publication Data
Names: Enz, Tammy, author.
Title: Awesome craft stick science / by Tammy Enz.
Description: North Mankato, Minnesota : Capstone Press, [2017] | Series: Edge
books. Recycled science | Audience: Ages 9-15.? | Audience: Grades 4 to 6.? | Includes
bibliographical references and index.
Identifiers: LCCN 2015045733|
ISBN 9781515708612 (library binding) |
ISBN 9781515708650 (eBook PDF)
Subjects: LCSH: Craft sticks—Juvenile literature. | Handicraft—Equipment and supplies—
Juvenile literature. | Recycling (Waste, etc.)—Juvenile literature. | CYAC: Handicraft. | Recycling
(Waste)
Classification: LCC TT880 .E69 2017 | DDC 745.5—dc23
LC record available at http://lccn.loc.gov/2015045733

Editorial Credits
Brenda Haugen, editor; Russell Griesmer, designer; Tracy Cummins, media specialist;
Kathy McColley, production specialist

Photo Credits
Capstone Studio: Karon Dubke (All images except the following); Shutterstock: Georgios Kollidas, 23

Design elements provided by Shutterstock: bimka, FINDEEP, fourb, Golbay, jannoon028, mexrix,
Picsfive, Sarunyu_foto, STILLFX, Your Design

Printed and bound in the USA.
009696F16

TABLE OF CONTENTS

AWESOME CRAFT
STICK SCIENCE

STICK AROUND!

There's nothing like a tasty snack on a stick. But when you finish smacking that snack, don't discard the stick. Repurpose it! Do more than repurpose it. Reveal science at work with awesome craft stick science projects. Their unique shape and material properties make them ideal for science projects. So eat up. Then gather some tools and get to work! (Don't forget that jumbo craft sticks make awesome projects too.)

HAPPY ACCIDENT

More than 2 billion Popsicles are sold each year. But did you know their invention was accidental? Eleven-year-old Frank Epperson discovered the treat in 1905. He left his sugary drink with a stir stick outside overnight. After a chilly night, he found his drink frozen into a Popsicle.

WOODEN CHAIN

Did you ever wonder how curved wooden furniture is made? Usually bending a wood craft stick causes it to snap. But you can unlock the secret to bending wood with this experiment.

BRANCH OF SCIENCE: **BIOLOGY**
CONCEPT: **PROPERTIES OF WOOD**

YOU'LL NEED:

PUT IT TOGETHER:

STEP 1: Fill the cooker half full of water. Place the craft sticks inside. Cook for one to two hours at medium heat.

STEP 2: Carefully remove a stick with tongs. Allow the stick to cool for about a minute before touching it. Slowly begin bending the stick into a circle.

STEP 3: Fit the circle inside a cap. Repeat with the other sticks and caps.

STEP 4: Leave the sticks inside the caps overnight. Remove them, and carefully fit the links together to form a chain.

STEP 3   STEP 4

REUSABLE KNOWLEDGE:

Wood is a hygroscopic material. It can absorb water from its environment. The cells that make up wood have cellulose in their cell walls. Cellulose gives wood its strength. Dry wood is strong but brittle. Water makes cellulose soft and easy to stretch.

STRUCTURE OF WOOD

Live trees contain lots of water. Up to two-thirds of a tree's weight comes from the water inside of it. The water keeps the cell walls soft, allowing the tree to bend and sway without breaking.

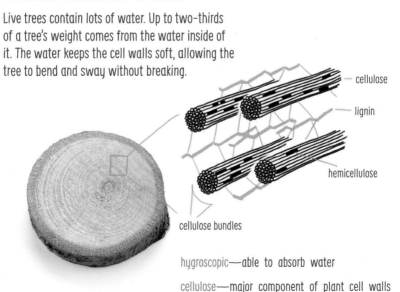

cellulose

lignin

hemicellulose

cellulose bundles

hygroscopic—able to absorb water

cellulose—major component of plant cell walls

CRYSTAL SNOWFLAKE

This chemistry experiment appears almost magical. Sparkling crystals appear overnight from clear liquid. Give it a try!

BRANCH OF SCIENCE: CHEMISTRY
CONCEPT: SUPER SATURATED SOLUTION

YOU'LL NEED:

- Pipe cleaner (any color)
- Scissors
- 6-inch (15-centimeter) long piece of string
- Craft stick
- Large drinking glass or jar
- 1.5 cups (.35 liter) boiling water
- 3 tablespoons (45 grams) of borax
- Spoon

SAFETY FIRST:

Have an adult help out when using hot water.

PUT IT TOGETHER:

STEP 1: Cut the pipe cleaner into three equal length sections. Twist the pieces together at their centers. Spread out the pieces to form a six-pointed asterisk.

STEP 2: Tie one end of the string around the top of the asterisk. Tie the other end around the center of the craft stick.

STEP 3: Lay the craft stick across the top of the glass, hanging the asterisk inside the glass. Adjust the string so the asterisk hangs about halfway down the glass.

STEP 4: Remove the asterisk, and pour the boiling water into the glass. Slowly stir in the borax powder.

STEP 5: Replace the asterisk inside the glass. Place the project somewhere it won't be disturbed. Leave it alone overnight, observing it often.

STEP 1

STEP 3

STEP 2

REUSABLE KNOWLEDGE:

In this experiment you created a super saturated liquid. By heating the water, you added energy. The energy caused water molecules to speed up. They collided with borax crystals, dissolving them. Hot water can dissolve more than cold water. So when the water cooled, there was no room for the extra borax. It returned to its solid form. The pipe cleaner was an easy place for the borax to cling.

WHAT IS BORAX?

Borax is a natural mineral that dissolves easily in water. It is found in dry lake beds and has many uses. In ancient times it was used for preserving food and mummies. Ancient Chinese pottery makers used it in glazes. Today it is used in detergent and cleaning products. It is also used as a fire retardant and for tooth whitening.

super saturated—a solution dissolving more material than it normally can

molecule—the smallest particle of a substance with the properties of that substance

CHAIN REACTION

Do you like lining up dominoes just to watch them fall in a chain reaction? Then you'll love this experiment. It takes a little patience and help from a friend. But it creates lots of fun and a lesson in physics.

BRANCH OF SCIENCE: PHYSICS
CONCEPT: POTENTIAL AND KINETIC ENERGY

YOU'LL NEED:

- A pile of craft sticks (jumbo ones work best)
- A friend

SAFETY FIRST:

Wear eye protection when working on this project.

PUT IT TOGETHER:

STEP 1: Take four sticks and lay them on a flat surface in a square shape. Overlap their ends by about 2 inches (5 cm). Make sure one end of each stick is lapped under while its other end is lapped over adjacent sticks.

STEP 2: Slide the ends of the two sticks closest to you so their ends overlap forming a "V." Hold your thumb on the tip of the V.

STEP 3: Have a friend weave another stick over and under the sticks on your left side. If done correctly, the sticks will be difficult to weave, but will hold together.

STEP 4: Now have your friend do the same thing to the stick ends on your right.

STEP 5: Alternate back and forth from side to side. Weave the tips of the two outer-most sticks.

STEP 6: When you run out of sticks, count down. Let both ends of the weave go at the same time. Watch out!

STEP 3

REUSABLE KNOWLEDGE:

Most materials bounce back when bent. (Although if bent too far they'll snap.) The energy in these bent sticks is called potential energy. This energy is stored up, waiting to return the sticks to their normal shape. When you finally let go, the stored energy turns into movement. This moving energy is called kinetic energy.

potential energy—energy caused by position or arrangement

kinetic energy—energy of motion

BOW AND ARROW

This bow and arrow project is a ton of fun to build. It's even more fun to play with. Test out a physics fact, and have a blast at the same time!

BRANCH OF SCIENCE: PHYSICS
CONCEPT: ACCELERATION DUE TO GRAVITY

YOU'LL NEED:

- 12 craft sticks
- Ruler
- Pen
- Hot glue gun
- 5 corks
- Utility knife
- Rubber band
- 2 twist ties
- Unsharpened pencil
- A friend
- Stopwatch

SAFETY FIRST:

Have an adult help out when using hot glue and sharp tools such as a utility knife.

PUT IT TOGETHER:

STEP 1: Measure and mark with a pencil the center of each of the craft sticks.

STEP 2: Overlap the ends of two sticks to form a 120-degree angle. Hot glue them together.

STEP 3: Glue another stick to the end of one of these sticks at the same angle. You will form a bow shape.

STEP 4: Glue the ends of another stick to connect the center of one angled piece to the center of the middle piece.

STEP 5: Repeat Step 4 to connect the other angled piece to the middle piece.

STEP 6: Glue the ends of a sixth stick to connect the centers of the pieces added in steps 4 and 5.

STEP 7: Repeat steps 2-6 to make another bow shape.

STEP 8: Use the utility knife to cut a cork in half to make two shorter corks.

STEP 9: Repeat Step 8 with the other two corks.

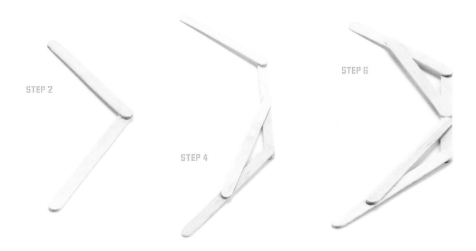

STEP 2

STEP 4

STEP 6

STEP 10: Sandwich five of the cork pieces between the bows. Glue them at the bow ends, at the angles, and in the center of the straight piece.

STEP 11: Stretch the rubber band between the bow ends. Connect each end of the rubber bands to a cork end with a twist tie.

STEP 12: To make the arrow, use the utility knife to slice a 0.125-inch (0.3-cm) wide slit in the pencil eraser.

STEP 13: Make a horizontal mark on a wall at about your shoulder height.

STEP 14: Rest the pencil on the center cork. Slide the eraser slit over the rubber band.

STEP 15: Holding the eraser, pull back the pencil. Release it perfectly horizontally, even with the mark on the wall. Have your friend time how long it takes to hit the ground.

STEP 16: Now have your friend time how long it takes for a pencil to hit the ground when you simply drop it from the height of the mark on the wall. How do the times compare?

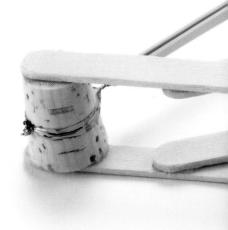

REUSABLE KNOWLEDGE:

Both pencils should hit the ground at nearly the same time. Why? The answer is gravity. One pencil moves horizontally and the other not at all. But gravity is pulling both downward at the same rate.

gravity—a force that pulls objects with mass together

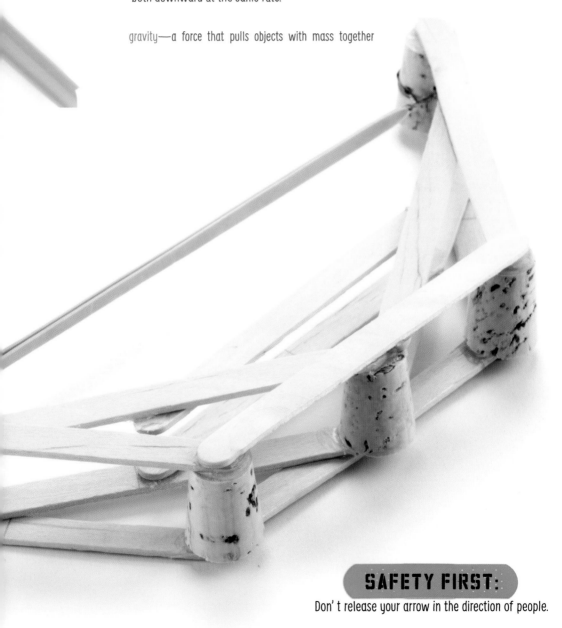

SAFETY FIRST:
Don't release your arrow in the direction of people.

HARMONICA

Do you like to make music, or at least really cool sounds? Try your hand at this project. It will give you more than a tune to play. It will give you a sense of how sound waves work.

BRANCH OF SCIENCE: **PHYSICS**
CONCEPT: **SOUND WAVES/PITCH**

YOU'LL NEED:

- 2 jumbo craft sticks
- Waxed paper
- Pen
- Scissors
- 2 rubber bands
- 2 wooden toothpicks

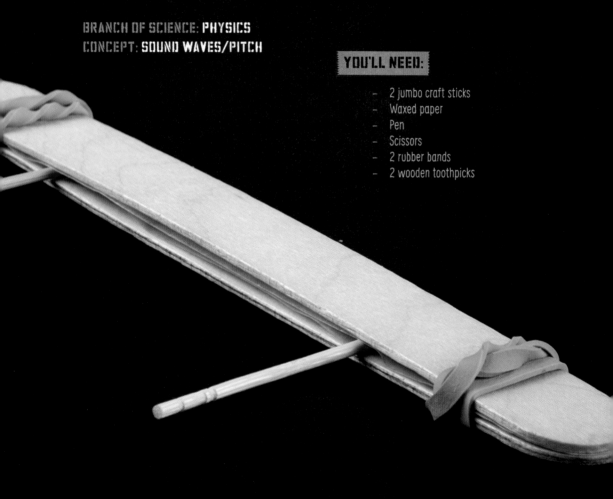

PUT IT TOGETHER:

STEP 1: Trace a craft stick onto the waxed paper with the pen. Cut out the shape. Repeat to make another piece.

STEP 2: Sandwich the waxed paper pieces between the sticks. Wrap rubber bands tightly about 0.5 inch (1 cm) from each end of the sticks.

STEP 3: Carefully insert the toothpicks between the waxed paper sheets. Slide one to each end, next to the rubber band.

STEP 4: Place the flat side of the harmonica between your lips. Blow gently in the center.

STEP 5: To change the sound, move the sticks farther from and then closer to the rubber bands.

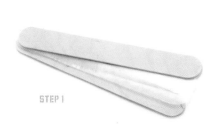

STEP 1

STEP 2

REUSABLE KNOWLEDGE.

Sound is caused by vibrations. People's vocal cords vibrate to make sounds. Parts of musical instruments also vibrate. The sound in this harmonica comes from vibrating waxed paper. The number of times that a sound wave vibrates in a certain period of time is its frequency. High-pitched sounds have high frequencies. Moving the toothpicks closer causes the paper to vibrate quicker. It creates a higher pitch.

Sound travels through the air at about 1,126 feet (340 meters) per second. It travels even faster in water. Sound must travel through a medium such as gas (air), water, or a solid object. Because there is no air on the moon, astronauts cannot hear each other talk there. They must use a radio.

frequency—number of waves passing a point in a certain amount of time

pitch—the highness or lowness of a sound

medium—a substance such as air or water through which sound waves pass

PADDLEBOAT

Have you ever watched a paddleboat churning through the water? This project will give you a look at how they work. Better yet, it will give you a look at how many things move. Newton's Third Law of Motion describes how fish, birds, and even rockets move.

BRANCH OF SCIENCE: PHYSICS
CONCEPT: NEWTON'S THIRD LAW OF MOTION

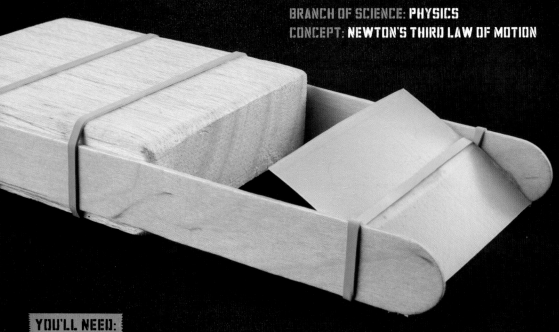

YOU'LL NEED:

- Piece of wood about 2 inches (5 cm) x 4 inches (10 cm) x 0.75-inch (2-cm) thick
- 2 jumbo craft sticks
- 3 rubber bands
- Hot glue gun
- Piece of plastic cut from a milk jug 1.5-inch (4-cm) square
- Pool or tub of water

SAFETY FIRST:

Have an adult help out when using hot glue.

PUT IT TOGETHER:

STEP 1: Place the flat sides of the craft sticks along the long sides of the block of wood. Allow their ends to stick about halfway past the end of the wood block.

STEP 2: Use two rubber bands to hold the sticks to the block of wood.

STEP 3: Place the third rubber band around the free ends of the sticks, 1 inch (2.5 cm) from their ends. Glue the rubber band to the outside faces of the sticks.

STEP 4: Place the plastic piece in the center of this rubber band. Holding the boat upright, wind the paddle several turns toward the back of the boat.

STEP 5: Place the boat in a tub, and release the paddle.

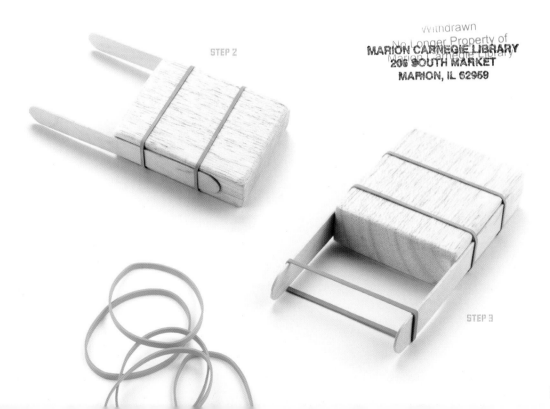

STEP 2

STEP 3

REUSABLE KNOWLEDGE:

When the paddle hits the water's surface it pushes water back. This causes the boat to move forward. This experiment displays Newton's Third Law of Motion. This law states that for every action there is an equal and opposite reaction. What happens if you hit a wall with your fist? The wall doesn't move backward due to your forward action. But it does push your fist back with the same force you exerted. You feel the force as a great big "ouch!"

SIR ISAAC NEWTON [1643-1727]

Sir Isaac Newton was a great scientist from the 1600s and 1700s. He is famous for his study of gravity. His three laws of motion form the basis for modern physics.

NEWTON'S LAWS

1. An object at rest stays at rest. A moving object will keep moving unless acted on. (Law of inertia)

2. Acceleration is produced when a force acts on a mass. Heavy objects take more force to move the same distance.

3. For every action there is an equal and opposite reaction.

HELICOPTER

Test this project outside or in a room with tall ceilings. Your helicopter sails high, giving you a peek at the science behind helicopter propellers.

BRANCH OF SCIENCE: **PHYSICS**
CONCEPT: **LIFT VERSUS GRAVITY**

YOU'LL NEED:

- Pan of boiling water
- Craft stick
- Tongs
- Heavy books
- Wooden skewer
- Sandpaper
- Hot glue gun
- 18 inch (46 cm) piece of string
- Empty thread spool

SAFETY FIRST:

Have an adult help out when using hot water and hot glue.

PUT IT TOGETHER:

STEP 1: Place the stick in the boiling water for about 10 minutes. Pull it out with the tongs. Hold it for several seconds while it cools.

STEP 2: Twist the ends in opposite directions. Place one end between upright books. Set heavy books on the other end to hold the twist in the stick. Allow the stick to dry for several hours.

STEP 3: Snap the skewer in half. Discard one half. Use the sandpaper to make the broken end of the other piece smooth and flat.

STEP 4: Use the hot glue to glue the flat end of the skewer piece to the center of the twisted craft stick.

STEP 5: Wrap the string around the skewer about 2 inches (5 cm) from its pointed end. Place this end into the center of the spool.

STEP 6: Holding the spool, grab the loose end of the string and pull it to launch the helicopter. (Practice winding the string in the opposite direction. Does the winding direction make a difference in how it flies?)

STEP 2

STEP 5

REUSABLE KNOWLEDGE:

Angled propellers move air faster across their tops than their bottoms. This creates suction, causing the propeller to lift. Spinning fast creates enough lift to overcome gravity.

FAST FACT:

Helicopters have one propeller on top and one on their tail. Why? The tail prop keeps the helicopter stable. Otherwise the helicopter would spin with the rotations of the main propeller.

CORK LAUNCHER

Build a rubber band launcher to bring some fun and excitement to you day! A rubber band's ability to stretch and spring gives this launcher its gusto. Whip up this project, and see the science behind a rubber band's power.

BRANCH OF SCIENCE: CHEMISTRY
CONCEPT: PROPERTIES OF ELASTOMERS

YOU'LL NEED:

- 4 jumbo craft sticks
- Hot glue gun
- 2 corks
- Utility knife
- Wooden clothespin
- 2 rubber bands

SAFETY FIRST:

Have an adult help out when using hot glue and sharp tools such as a utility knife. And never point your launcher at people or animals.

PUT IT TOGETHER:

STEP 1: Overlap the ends of two sticks by about 1 inch (2.5 cm). Hot glue them to make a longer stick. Repeat with the remaining two sticks.

STEP 2: Use the utility knife to slice one of the corks in half. You'll have two shorter corks.

STEP 3: Sandwich one of the cork halves between the ends of the sticks from step 1. Sandwich the uncut cork between their other ends. Glue the corks in place.

STEP 4: Place the launcher on one of its flat sides. Glue a flat side of the clothespin near the end with the uncut cork. Its legs should face up the slope.

STEP 5: Loop one end of a rubber band through the other. Tuck it inside its other end to form a knot. This will connect the rubber bands.

STEP 1

STEP 5

STEP 3

STEP 6: Wrap one of the rubber bands several times tightly around the end of the launcher opposite the clothespin. Leave the other rubber band trailing toward the clothespin.

STEP 7: Pull this rubber band back, and snap it into the mouth of the clothespin.

STEP 8: Place the remaining half cork near the mouth of the clothespin. Place it inside the rubber band loop.

STEP 9: To launch, press open the clothespin.

STEP 7-9

REUSABLE KNOWLEDGE:

Rubber bands are *elastomers*. Elastomers are tangled chains of molecules that straighten when stretched. They can be stretched to twice their original length before snapping back. When stretching a rubber band, you add energy to it. The energy is stored to launch your cork.

elastomer—rubbery, easily stretched material

ELASTOMERS

When stretching a rubber band, you untangle a chain of molecules.

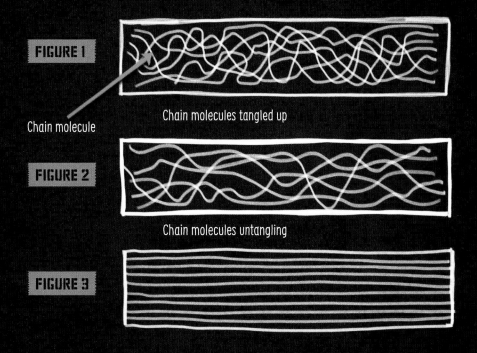

FIGURE 1

Chain molecule

Chain molecules tangled up

FIGURE 2

Chain molecules untangling

FIGURE 3

FAST FACT:

Rubber is harvested from the sap of rubber trees.

GLOSSARY

cellulose—major component of plant cell walls

elastomer—rubbery, easily stretched material

frequency—number of waves passing a point in a certain amount of time

gravity—a force that pulls objects with mass together

hygroscopic—able to absorb water

kinetic energy—energy of motion

medium—a substance such as air or water through which sound waves pass

molecule—the smallest particle of a substance with the properties of that substance

pitch—the highness or lowness of a sound

potential energy—energy caused by position or arrangement

super saturated—a solution dissolving more material than it normally can

READ MORE

Heinecke, Liz Lee. *Kitchen Science Lab for Kids: 52 Family Friendly Experiments from Around the House*. Beverly, Mass.: Quarry Books, 2014.

Leavitt, Loralee. *Candy Experiments*. Kansas City, Mo.: Andrews McMeel Publishing, 2012.

Leavitt, Loralee. *Candy Experiments 2*. Kansas City, Mo.: Andrews McMeel Publishing, 2014.

INTERNET SITES

FactHound offers a safe, fun way to find Internet sites related to this book. All of the sites on FactHound have been researched by our staff.

Here's all you do:
Visit *www.facthound.com*
Type in this code: 9781515708612

Check out projects, games and lots more at
www.capstonekids.com

CRITICAL THINKING USING THE COMMON CORE

1. Cite two properties of wood related to the fact that it comes from a plant. (Key Ideas and Details)

2. Potential energy is defined as energy due to position. Explain what this means. (Craft and Structure)

3. Refer the infographic on page 29 to explain how the molecular structure of an elastomer allows it to stretch to twice its length. (Integration of Knowledge and Ideas)

INDEX